VALERIAN AND LAURELINE

THE CITY OF SHIFTING WATERS

J.-C. MÉZIÈRES AND P. CHRISTIN
COLOUR WORK: E. TRANLÉ AND J.-C. MÉZIÈRES

9th CINEBOOK
The 9th Art Publisher

Original title: Valerian 1 – La cité des eaux mouvantes
Original edition: © Dargaud Paris, 1970 by Christin, Mezières & Tran-Lê
First published in *Pilote* magazine in 1968 - www.dargaud.com - All rights reserved
English translation: © 2010 Cinebook Ltd - Translator: Jerome Saincantin
Lettering and text layout: Imadjinn

This edition first published in Great Britain in 2010 by
Cinebook Ltd - 56 Beech Avenue - Canterbury, Kent - CT4 7TA
www.cinebook.com - Third printing: May 2016 - Printed in Spain by EGEDSA
A CIP catalogue record for this book is available from the British Library
ISBN 978-1-84918-038-2

WELL, THAT'S THE STRANGEST THING. HE SHOWED UP IN NEW YORK IN 1986... AND YOU'RE GOING TO FOLLOW HIM THERE...

YOU MUST BE KIDDING, SIR!

WHAT'S SO WEIRD ABOUT THAT?

LET ME EXPLAIN, MY YOUNG FRIEND. I SEE YOU DON'T KNOW EVERYTHING ABOUT GALAXITY'S HISTORY YET. ACTUALLY, NO ONE KNOWS EXACTLY WHAT HAPPENED IN OUR PAST BETWEEN 1986 AND THE 24TH CENTURY. IT'S A MYSTERIOUS ERA: THE DARK AGES OF THE EARTH. THAT WAS WHEN TRADITIONAL CIVILISATION WAS SWEPT AWAY BY A CATACLYSM...

HERE, LOOK AT THESE PICTURES: THEY WERE TAKEN FROM ONE OF THE PRIMITIVE SATELLITES THAT USED TO ORBIT THE EARTH BACK THEN. THEY'RE THE ONLY DOCUMENTS WE HAVE—AND THEY WERE DAMAGED BY RADIATION...

IN 1986, A HYDROGEN BOMB DEPOT LOCATED NEAR THE NORTH POLE ACCIDENTALLY BLEW UP. HERE YOU CAN SEE A SNAPSHOT OF THE EXPLOSION. THE ICECAPS IMMEDIATELY BEGAN TO MELT... THE CLIMATE BECAME MUCH HOTTER ALL ACROSS THE GLOBE, AND THE SEA LEVEL ROSE BY SEVERAL DOZEN FEET, SWALLOWING MOST LARGE CITIES...

EVERYTHING HAPPENED VERY QUICKLY! TWO WEEKS LATER, THE VERY SHAPE OF THE CONTINENTS HAD CHANGED BEYOND RECOGNITION. NATIONS HAD BROKEN UP; SCIENTIFIC ARCHIVES HAD BEEN LOST FOR EVER...

WASN'T IT DURING THOSE CURSED YEARS THAT SPACE-TIME TRAVEL WAS INVENTED— EVENTUALLY ALLOWING EARTH TO REBUILD ITS POWER?

SO IT IS SAID, VALERIAN, ALTHOUGH THE FIRST ACTUAL MACHINE DATES BACK TO 2314. BUT THE TIME IN BETWEEN IS SHROUDED IN COMPLETE SECRECY, SINCE THE CHARTER DRAFTED BY GALAXITY FORBIDS ALL TRAVEL TO THAT ERA. I'VE BEEN THINKING, THOUGH. THE SITUATION IS TOO SERIOUS: WE HAVE TO DISOBEY THE CHARTER... THEREFORE, I'M ASKING YOU TO GO AND SEARCH FOR XOMBUL...

BUT... SIR, THE ZONE IS FORBIDDEN; WE DON'T EVEN KNOW WHAT SHAPE THE RELAYS ARE IN! WHAT'LL HAPPEN IF MY SPACE-TIMER MATERIALISES UNDER 200 FEET OF WATER?

IT'S A RISK YOU'LL HAVE TO TAKE! SINCE THE AUTOMATIC SYSTEMS NOTIFIED US OF XOMBUL'S ARRIVAL, IT MEANS THAT THE RELAY'S STILL WORKING. YOU HAVE MY FULL CONFIDENCE! YOU'RE LEAVING IMMEDIATELY. I'M KEEPING LAURELINE HERE—IF NEEDED, SHE CAN GO INTO ACTION ONCE WE RECEIVE THE FIRST MESSAGE FROM YOU...

IF YOU EVER RECEIVE ONE!... OH, WELL, DON'T WORRY—I CAN SWIM...

BE CAREFUL, VALERIAN...

AND AFTER SOME QUICK PREPARATIONS, IN AN INSTANT VALERIAN'S SPACE-TIMER CROSSES THE CENTURIES SEPARATING GALAXITY FROM...

... NEW YORK, 1986!

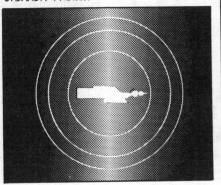

3

WELL, THE RELAY'S NOT QUITE A FISH TANK YET, BUT IT'S WELL ON ITS WAY TO BECOMING ONE! I'D BETTER GET OUT OF HERE QUICK...

EVERYTHING IS ROTTEN FROM THE DAMP. AND I WONDER WHERE THAT MUFFLED THUMPING IS COMING FROM...

BOM

BOM

3A

!?! OH, THAT'S GREAT! BRILLIANT CHOICE FOR THE RELAY'S LOCATION! HOW AM I GOING TO MAKE MY WAY OUT? I'D BETTER THINK HARD.

WHAT...? THE STATUE IS COLLAPSING!

3B

4

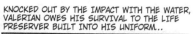

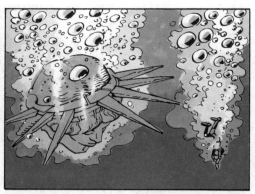

KNOCKED OUT BY THE IMPACT WITH THE WATER, VALERIAN OWES HIS SURVIVAL TO THE LIFE PRESERVER BUILT INTO HIS UNIFORM...

AND MUCH LATER...

HEY...

LOOK OVER THERE!... THERE'S A GUY IN THE DRINK... MIGHT BE ONE OF OURS. HEAD FOR HIM...

YOU KNOW THIS GUY, BUD?

NEVER SEEN HIM BEFORE! WE'LL SORT THIS OUT LATER. COME ON, LET'S GO BACK... THE SEA IS GOING TO GET EVEN WORSE WITH NIGHTFALL! WHAT ROTTEN WEATHER, DAMMIT!...

IS HE ALIVE AT LEAST?

YEAH, BUT HE'S OUT COLD...

IN THE FLOODED STREETS OF NEW YORK, THE LAUNCH SLOWLY THREADS ITS WAY THROUGH THE UNHEALTHFUL VEGETATION THAT FLOURISHES IN THE SWELTERING HEAT...

ALFONSO, YOU TIE HIM UP AND LEAVE HIM IN THE TWELFTH-FLOOR STOREROOM... WE'LL TAKE CARE OF HIM LATER! WE'RE LEAVING IN TWO MINUTES TO FINISH THE WORK...

OK, BUD, WE'LL BE RIGHT BACK!

5A

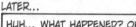

LATER...

HUH... WHAT HAPPENED? OH, YEAH... THE STATUE COLLAPSED... THE DIVE... AND NOW I'M ALL TRUSSED UP IN HERE...

MUST BE THE FOOD SECTION IN A DEPARTMENT STORE... EVERYTHING LOOKS TRASHED!

WHOEVER IT WAS THAT DUMPED ME INSIDE THIS RATHOLE, I HAVE TO GET OUT...

JUST A LITTLE PATIENCE... THIS WILL DO...

A FEW MINUTES LATER...

THERE, THAT'S DONE! AND IT SOUNDS LIKE IT WAS JUST IN TIME—I'M ABOUT TO HAVE GUESTS...

5B

SO! WE CAN HAVE A LITTLE CHAT WITH OUR FLOATING SURVIVOR AT LAST...

WITH ANY LUCK, I'LL FIND OUT WHAT THIS IS ALL ABOUT...

HEY, NUTS: ALFONSO TOLD YOU THAT'S WHERE HE'D LEFT THE GUY, RIGHT?... SO WHERE IS HE???

WHAT?! YOU DON'T REMEMBER?!! MAN, YOU'RE LOSING IT COMPLETELY, NUTS!... I'M WARNING YOU...

FORGET IT, BUD! IF WE WANT TO FINISH CLEANING UP THE FIFTH AVENUE JEWELLERS TODAY, WE'D BETTER GET A MOVE ON!

GOT IT... THESE CLOWNS ARE RANSACKING THE CITY! NOTHING TO DO WITH XOMBUL...

... I'M OUT OF HERE! HEY!

WHOA! LOOK AT THE STRANGE RATS YOU FIND AROUND HERE!!!

LET'S GET HIM!!!

ANOTHER FLOOR OR TWO AND I SHOULD BE AT WATER LEVEL. PERHAPS I'LL MANAGE TO SHAKE THEM OFF!

MOMENTS LATER AND A FEW FLOORS DOWN...

MACY'S 4th FLOOR

BUD! I SAW SOMETHING PASS BY THE WINDOW... HE MUST HAVE DIVED!

WHERE THE HELL DID THAT GUY GO?

THERE! THAT'S HIM!

LET'S GET THE LAUNCH!!

TWO FLOORS UP...

THEY BOUGHT IT! NO NEED TO THROW ANOTHER DUMMY... ESPECIALLY A BRIDE... AND NOW, LET'S VAMOOSE!

DAMN! A DUMMY IN A WEDDING TUX!

WE'VE BEEN HAD!

NO! LOOK OVER THERE!

SHOOT HIM, NUTS!

THE ROOF! I HAVE TO GET TO THE ROOF TO ESCAPE!

VALERIAN SLOWLY MAKES HIS WAY THROUGH THE JUNGLE THAT COVERS THE ROOFTOPS OF THE OLD BUILDINGS, UNTIL...

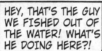

HEY, THAT'S THE GUY WE FISHED OUT OF THE WATER! WHAT'S HE DOING HERE?!

HEY, STOP!

NOT SO FAST, PALS—YOU DON'T HAVE ME JUST YET!

8A

A LITTLE WHILE LATER...

WELL! I MADE IT THROUGH TODAY, BUT TALK ABOUT A WELCOMING COMMITTEE! AND NONE OF THIS HELPED ME GET ANY CLOSER TO XOMBUL. THE CITY LOOKS COMPLETELY DESERTED, MY WOULD-BE RESCUERS ASIDE... EVEN THE EMPIRE STATE BUILDING IS DEAD. HEY... THAT'S THE TALLEST BUILDING IN MIDTOWN MANHATTAN... THIS GIVES ME AN IDEA...

I LOST MY GUN!! BUT WE'RE NOT DONE, YOU AND ME!

ALFONSO, WE'D BETTER GO GET SOME REINFORCEMENTS...

8B

9

SEVERAL DOZEN FLOORS UP, AT THE TOP OF THE EMPIRE STATE BUILDING...

STILL, IF ANYTHING'S GOING ON SOMEWHERE IN THIS AREA, HERE'S WHERE I HAVE THE BEST CHANCE OF FINDING OUT...

THIS CITY'S GOING TO GIVE ME A HEART ATTACK... 2820 STEPS... THAT'S TOUGH, EVEN FOR AN AGENT OF SPACE-TIME...

PITCH BLACK... LET'S SEE OVER THIS WAY!...

HEY! A LIGHT!

9A

INTERESTING!... THERE'S A LIGHT ON THE TOP FLOOR OF THE UNITED NATIONS BUILDING!... AND YET THERE'S NO POWER IN NEW YORK! THIS ISN'T THE STYLE OF MY EARLIER GANGSTERS. NOTHING TO LOSE BY GOING THERE TO HAVE A CLOSER LOOK!

GREAT, MORE STEPS... BUT NO WAY I'M SWIMMING TO THE UN; I NEED SOME KIND OF RAFT!...

AND AFTER SOME TIME SPENT SEARCHING FRUITLESSLY...

HO HO! THE BOARD MEMBERS HAD QUITE A COMFY SETUP HERE!...

... I THINK A CEO'S CHAIR WILL DO ME JUST FINE!

9B

10

IT WAS DEFINITELY WORTH IT! WHO ARE THESE WEIRDOES BUSY PILLAGING SCIENTIFIC ARCHIVES!?!... BY BETELGEUSE!... THEY'RE...

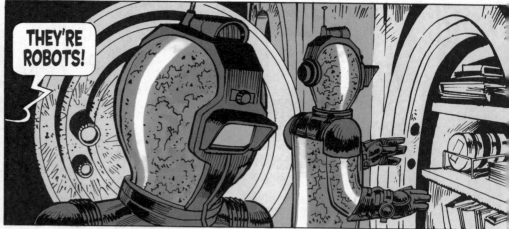

THEY'RE ROBOTS!

AND SOON...

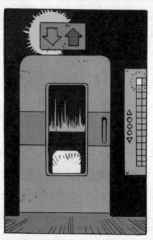

GROUND FLOOR!... THE ELEVATOR IS BELOW SEA LEVEL!!!

ONLY ONE THING TO DO... FIND MYSELF SOME DIVING EQUIPMENT AND GO TO WHERE THE ELEVATOR STOPS! I DON'T KNOW IF XOMBUL IS BEHIND THIS, BUT IT LOOKS LIKE I HAVE AN INTERESTING LEAD!...

LATER...

HEY! LOOK WHO'S COMING! I'LL BE DAMNED!!!

WATCH THIS. THIS'LL BE A GOOD LAUGH!

POP
POP

HEY?

SHPAM

ALL RIGHT, GET IN! ENOUGH OF YOUR LITTLE NIGHTLY EXCURSIONS!... YOU AIN'T TOO SMART AFTER ALL...

I WAS PLANNING TO DO YOU IN; BUT SINCE WE'RE A BIT SHORT-HANDED, YOU'RE GOING TO MAKE YOURSELF USEFUL...

HA HA HA!!!

PLOP PLOP PLOP PLOP

SO, DID THE LOSERS FROM THE "AUTHORITIES IN EXILE" SEND YOU, THEN? YOU CAME TO SPY ON US, DIDN'T YOU? WELL, YOU'RE IN FOR A TREAT! OF COURSE, ONCE WE'RE DONE: BOOM... ONE TO THE HEAD. BUT UNTIL THEN, YOU'LL HAVE PLENTY TO SEE. DON'T YOU WORRY...

YOU KNOW, AS FAR AS I'M CONCERNED, YOU CAN GRAB ANYTHING YOU WANT! LET'S MAKE A DEAL: I LEAVE YOU ALONE, AND YOU DO THE SAME...

TSK TSK... SEE, WE'VE GOT OUR HANDS ON A NICE, FAT PILE OF LOOT! EVERY RICH CAT IN NEW YORK CITY RAN AT THE FIRST BIG WAVE—AND LEFT THEIR SAVINGS BEHIND... BELIEVE ME, THERE'S A LOT OF STUFF IN THE MUSEUMS, AND PLENTY OF CASH IN THE BANKS... SO, EVEN IF IT WASN'T THE COPS THAT SENT YOU, THERE'S NO WAY WE'RE GIVING YOU A CHANCE TO RAT ON US...

AS THE CRAFT KEEPS GOING UP FIFTH AVENUE TOWARDS CENTRAL PARK, THE SUN BEGINS TO RISE...

YEAH... IT'S THE BIGGEST HEIST EVER! AND THERE ISN'T MUCH RISK INVOLVED, 'CAUSE THOSE CHICKEN COPS WERE THE FIRST TO BUG OUT! SOMETIMES, WHEN THERE'S NO STORM, THE NAVY LAUNCHES ONE OF THE FEW PLANES IT'S GOT LEFT FROM ITS LAST WORKING CARRIER AND SENDS IT TO PATROL OVER NEW YORK. BUT IT'S ALL FOR SHOW... THERE ISN'T EVEN A REAL GOVERNMENT LEFT ANYWHERE...

AND... YOU HAVE PLANS?

SURE DO, BUDDY! ONCE THE HOLDS ARE FULL, THE BIG BOSS IS TAKING US WITH HIM. HE PROMISED US THE GOOD LIFE. AND BELIEVE ME, WHEN YOU SEE SUN RAE, YOU'LL UNDER-STAND WHY WE'RE WITH HIM...

12A

LOOK AT THAT! THE ONLY CARGO SHIP THAT DIDN'T SINK AT ITS MOORING WHEN THE WATER BEGAN TO RISE. WE SCROUNGED UP EVERY GALLON OF OIL LEFT IN NEW YORK. ANOTHER FEW DAYS TO FINISH LOADING UP AND WE'LL RAISE ANCHOR... AS RICH MEN! HA! HA! HA!

IT'S MORNING AT THE LOOTERS' HQ—THE GRAND PLAZA HOTEL...

THAT'S SUN RAE OVER THERE... YOU'D BETTER NOT DISTURB HIM WHILE HE'S PLAYING. HE'S MERCILESS WHEN THAT HAPPENS... NOW MOVE—YOU'RE GOING TO JOIN THE OTHER PRISONERS...

12B

THE DAYS GO BY, FILLED WITH EXHAUSTING LABOUR. THE HEAT IS MORE AND MORE OPPRESSIVE. STEADY RAIN STOPS ONLY FOR SUDDEN SQUALLS, AND THE WATER KEEPS RISING...

GET A MOVE ON, YOU LAZY BUMS. IT'S THE ROCKEFELLERS' SILVERWARE—SHOW SOME RESPECT, WILL YOU?

SEE THESE GOLD BRICKS? I GOT THEM FROM THE CHASE MANHATTAN BANK! IT'S NOT EASY TO CRACK A SAFE UNDER 10 FEET OF WATER!

... NO KIDDING! ME, I GOT ZIP. JUST A FEW HALF-ROTTED HUNDRED-DOLLAR BILLS...

HEY!

WHAT DO YOU THINK OF MY STATUE, EH? ME, I LIKE MUSEUMS BEST...

IT'S PRETTY, ISN'T IT?...

YOU SICK FOOL!... WE TOLD YOU BEFORE: WHAT'S IMPORTANT IS JEWELS... HE GETS CRAZIER ALL THE TIME, THAT GUY!...

ENOUGH TIME WASTED WITH YOUR CRAP... HEY! YOU OVER THERE... COME AND THROW THIS OVERBOARD...

PLOOF

THE AFTERNOON OF THE SAME DAY...

HO, DOWN THERE! ALL HANDS ON DECK! IT'S A STORM! THE SHIP'S BREAKING FROM ITS MOORING...

HMM! IT'S NOW OR NEVER!

14

WELL! RATS LEAVING THE SINKING SHIP?

AAAAH!... THAT FEELS GOOD!

NO NEED TO ADVERTISE MY DEPARTURE... COME HERE, YOU!

HEY, THERE'S SOMEONE IN HERE!

14A

THAT ONE'S SMALL BUT TOUGH!...

SOON, THE RAFT IS FLOATING AWAY THROUGH THE AILING TREES OF CENTRAL PARK...

OK, VALERIAN, THAT'S ENOUGH FOR TODAY... BESIDES, YOU SEEM SOMEWHAT OFF YOUR GAME!!!

LAURELINE! WHAT ARE YOU DOING HERE?!?

NOW'S NOT THE TIME FOR QUESTIONS! FOLLOW ME—I HAVE A DINGHY WAITING!

14B

LET'S STOP HERE...

SINCE I FOUND THIS LITTLE APARTMENT IN GREENWICH VILLAGE, I'VE GROWN FOND OF IT. IT'S THE ONLY NICE PLACE IN THE WHOLE CITY...

MM'YEAH, NOT BAD, NOT BAD... BUT HOW ABOUT YOU TELL ME HOW YOU CAME TO BE HERE?

ELEMENTARY, MY FRIEND... WITH NO NEWS FROM YOU, I ARRIVED THROUGH THE BRASILIA RELAY FOUR DAYS AGO. THAT SAME EVENING, I CONVINCED THE FORMER PRESIDENT TO LEND ME HIS PERSONAL JET—EVEN THOUGH IT WAS THE LAST REMNANT OF HIS AUTHORITY.

AFTER GETTING HERE, I HID THE PLANE IN A SUBURB OF NEW YORK... ONE DAY TO UNDERSTAND THE SITUATION, TWO DAYS TO LOCATE YOU AND WAIT FOR THE RIGHT TIME—AND HERE WE ARE...

THE CHEEK OF THESE SPATIO-TEMPORAL AGENT CHICKS!!! YOU KNOW, I ALWAYS THOUGHT THE SERVICE SHOULD BE EXCLUSIVELY FOR US MEN—YOU'RE ALL TOO SMART FOR US... WHAT ARE YOU WORKING ON NOW, ANYWAY?

HA HA! YOU'LL SEE WHY WE GET ACCEPTED INTO YOUR PRESTIGIOUS ORGANISATION...

... IT'S BECAUSE **WE** CAN COOK! AND HOW! SEE HOW ELEGANTLY THESE TINS WERE OPENED, HMMM?... DINNER IS SERVED!

A FEW TINS LATER...

YES, THE SITUATION IS HORRIBLE. MILLIONS OF PEOPLE DIED IN THE TSUNAMIS OR FROM RADIATION, BUT THERE ARE MILLIONS MORE WHO TOOK REFUGE ANYWHERE THEY COULD— IN THE HILLS, IN THE MOUNTAINS, ON FLOATING HOUSES...

WHEN THEY DON'T DIE OF STARVATION OR DISEASE, I'VE BEEN TOLD THEY'LL KILL EACH OTHER FOR JUST ABOUT ANYTHING: A BAG OF SUGAR OR A CAN OF PETROL...

WHAT ABOUT GOVERNMENTS?

LOOKS LIKE IT'S THE SAME THING EVERYWHERE: EITHER THE PEOPLE IN CHARGE VANISHED OR SOME GANGSTER USED THE SITUATION TO SEIZE CONTROL...

... IN ANY CASE, INFORMATION IS SCARCE. COMMUNICATIONS ARE SEVERED, AND ALMOST ALL RADIOS ARE DEAD.

AND IN BRASILIA? SAME THING?

NO, NOT QUITE. THE AUTHORITIES ARE PANICKING, INCLUDING MY LITTLE BUDDY THE FORMER PRESIDENT, WHO'S HIDING IN HIS PALACE. BUT, AS CHANCE HAD IT, THERE WAS A GREAT SYMPOSIUM THAT GATHERED SCIENTISTS AND WRITERS FROM ALL AROUND THE WORLD...

... WHEN THE FIRST TSUNAMI HIT. THEY ALL STAYED THERE AND ARE TRYING TO SAVE WHAT THEY CAN. THEIR WORST FEAR IS THAT, BY NOW, ALL SCIENTIFIC ARCHIVES MUST HAVE BEEN IRRETRIEVABLY LOST. IN MANY AREAS, THEY'LL HAVE TO START OVER FROM SCRATCH.

DID YOU SAY SCIENTIFIC ARCHIVES?

LISTEN! DURING MY INVESTIGATIONS HERE, I HAPPENED UPON SOME STRANGE FOLKS WHO WERE HAPPILY PILLAGING THE UN SCIENTIFIC LIBRARY. RIGHT FROM THE START, I THOUGHT XOMBUL COULD BE BEHIND THAT...

... AND THE MORE I THINK ABOUT IT, THE MORE LOGICAL IT BECOMES. YOU JUST GAVE ME THE KEY TO THE RIDDLE. IN A WORLD IN SUCH A TERRIBLE STATE AS THIS ONE, WHO'S GOING TO GRAB THE REAL POWER? NOT THE POLITICIANS, NOT THE GANGSTERS...

THE ONLY ONES WHO CAN ACT WILL BE THE BRAINS, AND ESPECIALLY THOSE WITH THE POWER OF SCIENCE BEHIND THEM!!! AND THAT'S SOMETHING THAT I'M SURE XOMBUL—WITH HIS THIRST FOR POWER AND HIS DREAMS OF CHANGING EARTH'S HISTORY—HAS ALREADY THOUGHT OF!

DO YOU THINK YOU CAN PICK UP HIS TRAIL?

NOT WITHOUT HELP. FIRST, WE'LL NEED SOME DIVING EQUIPMENT TO FIND THE ELEVATOR USED BY THOSE ROBOTS I SAW. BESIDES, I CAN'T BE CERTAIN IT WAS XOMBUL WHO WAS CONTROLLING THEM.

ANYWAY, WHAT WE NEED TO INCREASE OUR CHANCES IS AN ALLY. COME ON, LET'S GO!

GO... WHERE?

TO SEE SUN RAE, THE LEADER OF THE GANG YOU RESCUED ME FROM!

AFTER BORROWING FROM A 20TH CENTURY WARDROBE, VALERIAN AND LAURELINE ARE SOON HIDING ABOARD THE LOOTERS' CARGO SHIP. IN THE BUSTLE OF FINAL LOADING, NO ONE NOTICES THEM. AND...

SUN RAE'S ALONE... AS SOON AS THE OTHERS ARE OFF THE SHIP, WE'RE GOING IN!

SUN RAE, YOU'RE OUR PRISONER... FOR A LITTLE WHILE. I NEED TO SPEAK WITH YOU.

!

HA HA HA!
REBELS! DO YOU HAVE ANY IDEA OF THE RISK YOU'RE TAKING?... GO ON, SPEAK! AND THIS HAD BETTER BE GOOD. OTHERWISE... HA HA!

LATER...

I'VE LISTENED. NOW, WHAT DO YOU PROPOSE?

THIS: THE WATER'S RISING. SOON, YOU'LL BE FORCED TO LEAVE NEW YORK. WHEREVER YOU GO, WHAT GOOD WILL YOUR TREASURES AND YOUR MONEY BE? NO ONE'S GOT ANYTHING TO BUY OR SELL...

IF YOU WANT TO BE IN CHARGE, YOU'LL SUCCEED BY KNOWING MORE THAN THE OTHERS. JOIN ME IN FINDING THE BEINGS I TOLD YOU ABOUT. I HAVE NO INTEREST IN THEIR SCIENTIFIC SECRETS. IN OTHER WORDS: TO YOU THE POWER, TO ME THE MAN I'M HUNTING.

THE NEXT MORNING, SUN RAE HAVING ACCEPTED VALERIAN'S DEAL, AN UNDERWATER CHASE BEGINS.
A FEW OF THE LOOTERS ARE ESCORTING THEIR BOSS AND THE TWO YOUNG SPATIO-TEMPORAL AGENTS, WHO HAD NO DIFFICULTY LOCATING THE ROBOTS AS THEY WERE COMING OUT OF THE UNITED NATIONS BUILDING...

IN THE SILENCE THAT HAS FOR EVER SETTLED INTO THE NEW YORK CITY SUBWAY TUNNELS, THE TAIL CONTINUES FROM A SAFE DISTANCE BEHIND THE ROBOTS.

AT LAST, FOLLOWING THE MACHINES UP AN OLD VENTILATION SHAFT...

18

DAMMIT! WHICH ONE OF THESE CORRIDORS DID THOSE DAMNED ROBOTS TAKE?

LET'S SPLIT UP. YOU GO THAT WAY...

IF ONE GROUP ISN'T BACK HERE IN AN HOUR, THEN EVERY MAN FOR HIMSELF—GET BACK TO THE SHIP AND CAST OFF.

CAREFUL... WE'RE NOT HERE FOR A SHOOTOUT. JUST TO LOOK...

WELL, WE'LL SOON HAVE A CLEAR VIEW OF THINGS. WE'RE ALMOST OUTSIDE.

20A

THAT'S WHAT I THOUGHT! WE'RE IN WASHINGTON HEIGHTS, ONE OF THE HIGHEST POINTS IN MANHATTAN.

LOOK OVER THERE! THEY MUST HAVE GONE INSIDE THAT BUILDING!

20B

19

FROM THE TREE WE'LL BE ABLE TO SEE INSIDE...

AND THERE THEY ARE...

WHAT ARE THEY DOING?

WE'LL KNOW IN A MOMENT. WE HAVE TO GET INSIDE TO HEAR WHAT'S GOING ON!

CENTRAL LAB CALLING NEW YORK BASE... CENTRAL LAB CALLING NEW YORK BASE...

THIS IS CENTRAL LAB. HAVE YOU COMPLETED YOUR TASK IN THE UNITED NATIONS BUILDING?

MISSION ACCOMPLISHED, SIR!

XOMBUL! WELL, HOW ABOUT THAT!

WELL DONE! WHAT A GREAT DETECTIVE YOU ARE!

GOOD. THEN YOU WILL LEAVE IMMEDIATELY. WE'VE CALCULATED THAT THE LAST TSUNAMI WILL HIT NEW YORK CITY IN LESS THAN AN HOUR. THE REMNANTS OF THE ICECAP BROKE UP. BEFORE YOU DEPART, BLOW UP THE PLACE PER THE PLAN. I WANT NO TRACE OF YOUR EVER BEING THERE, UNDERSTOOD? **HEY, WHAT?...**

UP THERE! SOMEONE'S HIDING BEHIND THE PILLARS!

OK, TIME TO GO!

JUST WAIT A SECOND!

BAM

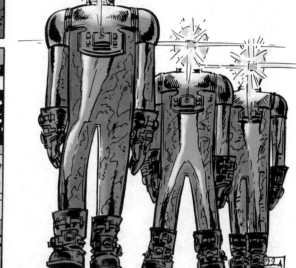

THIS IS THE CENTRAL LAB! TURN ON ANOTHER SCREEN, YOU IMBECILES. I CAN'T SEE A THING! **HURRY UP!**

NO! I'M STAYING! I'M NOT GOING TO LET THEM FRY US LIKE CHICKENS!

THEY HAVE DISINTEGRATORS!

WE'VE GOT TO RUN!

TAKE THEM ALIVE!

SAVE YOUR AMMO! THEY'RE IMPERVIOUS TO BULLETS!

I WANT THEM ALIVE! CAPTURE THEM! THEY CAN'T DO ANYTHING AGAINST YOU...

21

TRAPPED LIKE RATS! I CAN'T BELIEVE THIS!

SURRENDER!

NE PAKER

KNOWING THAT RESISTING WOULD BE POINTLESS, VALERIAN AND LAURELINE WALK TOWARDS THE SCREENS WHILE THE ROBOTS CARRY THE UNCONSCIOUS SUN RAE.

BY THE GALAXY!

IF IT ISN'T VALERIAN AND HIS INEVITABLE LITTLE GIRL!

HA HA HA!

... I DO SO LOVE THESE IMPROMPTU ENCOUNTERS! WELL, YOU'RE TOAST, VALERIAN. AND WHEN I SAY TOAST, I MEAN IN EVERY SENSE OF THE WORD... YOU'LL HAVE NOTICED WITH WHAT EASE MY... ER... ASSOCIATES CAN ROAST ANYTHING FROM AFAR... THEREFORE, I'D ADVISE YOU TO STAY PUT... BY THE WAY, WHO'S THAT BRUTE OF AN ACQUAINTANCE YOU HAVE NOW?

MY "ASSOCIATE," AS YOU PUT IT. BUT I HAVE BETTER TASTE THAN YOU IN THESE MATTERS: SUN RAE IS THE UNCONTESTED MASTER OF NEW YORK CITY, AND A FIRST-CLASS FLUTE PLAYER... WHEN HE'S NOT UNCONSCIOUS.

RIGHT... I SEE, ONE OF THE LOOTERS STILL ROAMING AROUND THE PLACE... WELL, YOU'RE ALL GOING TO JOIN ME HERE. UNDER CLOSE GUARD, BUT I DON'T WANT MY ASSOCIATES TO BE SEEN— THEY DO TEND TO STAND OUT, YOU SEE. SO, YOUR FLUTIST WILL PILOT THE HOVERCRAFT, SINCE HE KNOWS THE CITY SO WELL. OF COURSE, THERE WILL BE NO CONTACTING ANYONE. ONLY ONE ORDER: HEAD WEST. THE SLIGHTEST DEVIATION AND: PFFFIT... DISINTEGRATION, IS THAT CLEAR? NOW GO.. THE CATACLYSM COULD GET HERE ANY SECOND. HAVE A NICE TRIP! I TRUST THAT YOU'LL MAKE IT OUT ALL RIGHT... YOU DON'T HAVE A CHOICE!

THEY'RE NOT EVEN WATCHING US!

OH, THEY DON'T NEED TO! THEY KNOW WE'RE STUCK WITH THEM NOW—THE HOVERCRAFT IS OUR ONLY CHANCE.

OK, ALL RIGHT! LET GO OF ME! SO, I GATHER THAT YOU'VE FOUND WHAT YOU WERE LOOKING FOR?

ER... IN A WAY, YES. THE TRIP WILL SERVE MY PURPOSE. OF COURSE, IT DOESN'T SOUND LIKE AS GOOD A DEAL FOR YOU.

YOU THINK SO?...

?

IS EVERYONE THIS DENSE ON WHATEVER PLANET YOU CAME FROM? I DON'T GIVE A DAMN ABOUT THAT BUNCH OF PUNKS PILING UP DOLLARS INSIDE A TUB THAT'S PROBABLY GOING TO SINK IN A FEW MINUTES. I THINK THERE'S A LOT MORE TO GAIN FROM THIS... HOW DO YOU CALL HIM... XOMBUL!

... IF I COULD UNDERSTAND WHAT MAKES HIS "ASSOCIATES" TICK, I THINK I COULD DO SOME FANCY WORK WITH A GANG LIKE THAT... COME ON, WE'RE BOARDING.

READY?!

THE CRAFT CROSSES THE SWAMP AT REDUCED SPEED...

INSIDE THE COCKPIT WHERE THEY'RE STAYING QUIETLY OUT OF SIGHT, ONE OF THE ROBOTS OBEYS XOMBUL'S COMMAND AND...

... REMOTELY TRIGGERS THE DESTRUCTION OF THE BUNKER, WHICH BLOWS UP WITH A THUNDEROUS ROAR.

BOOM

AND THE POWERFUL MACHINE, ITS ENGINES RED-LINED, LEAPS FORWARD JUST ABOVE THE ROLLING WAVES, LASHED BY AN INCREASINGLY SAVAGE WIND...

UNDER THE SILENT BUT WATCHFUL SURVEILLANCE OF THE ROBOTS, IT'S ABOUT TO GO THROUGH NEW YORK CITY AND HEAD WEST...

LOOK, OVER THERE!

A WATERSPOUT!

INSIDE A NEW YORK CITY OPEN TO THE FURY OF THE ELEMENTS, A RACE AGAINST THE CLOCK BEGINS. IT IS RUN BY SUN RAE, WHOSE HERCULEAN STRENGTH AND KNOWLEDGE OF THE CITY SEEM TO MAKE A MOCKERY OF OBSTACLES.

THIS THING HANDLES LIKE A DREAM!

PREFERRING TO AVOID THE FRAGILE, SHAKING HIGH-RISES, SUN RAE IS FORCED TO CHOOSE OPEN SPACES. THE MACHINE PLOUGHS THROUGH THE THICK CARPET OF ALGAE THAT PROLIFERATES ABOVE THE OLD PARKS...

BUT SUDDENLY...

DAMN! I CAN'T SEE A THING WITH ALL THIS CRAP ON THE WINDSHIELD!

WATCH OUT, SUN RAE!
THE WAVE IS HERE! ALL OF DOWNTOWN IS TUMBLING DOWN!

OK! WE'LL TRY TO GET OUT AT WASHINGTON BRIDGE!

AND WHEN THE HOVERCRAFT ARRIVES NEAR THE BRIDGE...

UNDER THE TERRIFIC PRESSURE EXERTED BY THE TSUNAMI AS IT SWALLOWS THE CITY, THE POWERFUL STEEL CABLES OF THE SUSPENDED BRIDGE SNAP.

MIRACULOUSLY, THE CRAFT MANAGES TO CROSS THE HUDSON RIVER, LEAVING BEHIND A WRECK OF TWISTED METAL THAT SINKS BENEATH THE WAVES...

NO WAY WE CAN CROSS ANYWHERE... THE ONLY SOLUTION IS TO GO OVER THE BRIDGE!

HOURS GO BY. HAVING LEFT NEW YORK CITY FAR BEHIND, THE HOVERCRAFT TRAVELS ON THROUGH RUINED AREAS... EVERYWHERE, THE NOW-PASSED TSUNAMI HAS WREAKED HAVOC...

HELP!

STOP, PLEASE!

MURDERERS!! THEY'RE ABANDONING US!

THIS IS HORRIBLE, VALERIAN... ALL THOSE POOR PEOPLE.

YES, BUT WHAT CAN WE DO?... NOW THAT THE ROBOTS HAVE SWITCHED ON THE AUTOPILOT, WE DON'T EVEN KNOW WHERE WE'RE GOING...

LOOK AT WHAT'S LEFT OF CIVILISATION: A HALF-RUINED CAPITOL, AND ALL THESE BEAUTIFUL HOUSES TURNED INTO DESERTED ISLANDS...

YES, IT'S THE END OF A WORLD. AND WE'RE THE ONLY ONES TO KNOW THAT ANOTHER ONE WILL BE BORN OUT OF ALL THIS MISERY. OUR WORLD... GALAXITY'S WORLD...

THE HOVERCRAFT FORGES ON THROUGH THE CLAMMY AIR. STILL HEADING WEST, THE STRANGE CREW SAILS TOWARDS THE ROCKY MOUNTAINS, WHERE XOMBUL HAS ESTABLISHED HIS LAIR...

EVENTUALLY, A SWIFT CHANGE OF VEHICLE TAKES PLACE AT THE FOOT OF THE ROCKY MOUNTAINS, IN THE HEAVY ATMOSPHERE OF AN IMMINENT STORM. THE GROUP MADE UP OF VALERIAN, LAURELINE, SUN RAE AND XOMBUL'S CREATURES FINDS ITSELF INSIDE AN OLD ARMY HELICOPTER—AND READY TO FLY OVER THE FORBIDDING OBSTACLE...

THE HELICOPTER, PILOTED BY ONE OF THE ROBOTS, IS QUICKLY CAUGHT IN THE STORM...

UNDER THE CRASH OF LIGHTNING, IT THREADS ITS WAY BETWEEN ROCK WALLS...

... AT LAST, AFTER A DIFFICULT FLIGHT, IT MANAGES TO ESCAPE THE MOUNTAINS.

FUNNY, THIS LAND-SCAPE... I HAVE THE FEELING I'VE SEEN IT BEFORE!

ME, TOO! THIS GEYSER LOOKS FAMILIAR. UNLESS IT APPEARED AFTER THE DISASTER...

NO, NO... IT WAS THERE LONG BEFORE! WE'RE ABOVE YELLOWSTONE PARK, IN WYOMING! WHICH ALSO EXPLAINS THE BUFFALOS—IT'S THE LARGEST RESERVE OF WILD ANIMALS IN THE UNITED STATES...

THEIR TRIP COMPLETE, THE PASSENGERS HEAD INTO A CAVE. ONLY THREE OF THE ROBOTS STAY BEHIND AND BEGIN UNLOADING THE DOCUMENTS SNATCHED FROM NEW YORK CITY.

... THE JOURNEY CONTINUES UNTIL THE GROUP ARRIVES AT THE ENTRANCE TO A VAST LABORATORY.

INSIDE THE MOUNTAIN...

AH! THERE YOU ARE!

28

WELL, VALERIAN... WHO WOULD HAVE THOUGHT WE'D MEET AGAIN IN 1986! THE LAST TIME WE SAW EACH OTHER, WE WERE OLDER BY A FEW CENTURIES AND I WAS YOUR PRISONER.
A VERY UNPLEASANT SITUATION, YOU KNOW! FORTUNATELY, I STILL HAD A FEW ALLIES WHO LATER GOT ME OUT OF THAT PREDICAMENT...

THAT'S GOOD TO KNOW! I'LL HAVE TO TAKE CARE OF THEM WHEN I GET BACK!

OH, YOU KNOW, I'D BE SURPRISED IF YOU EVER WENT BACK TO WHERE YOU CAME FROM. BESIDES, I TOOK CARE TO DISPOSE OF THOSE COMPROMISING FRIENDS.

WHAT WAS ALL THAT JAZZ ABOUT?! I WISH I COULD UNDERSTAND...

FORGET IT! IT'S BUSINESS BETWEEN VALERIAN AND XOMBUL. AND IT'S A LITTLE COMPLICATED...

NO, NO... HE'S RIGHT! I DIDN'T BRING YOU HERE SO WE COULD DISCUSS THE PAST—OR MORE ACCURATELY, THE FUTURE. THE PRESENT IS MUCH TOO INTERESTING FOR THAT! COME, I'LL INTRODUCE YOU TO THE ONLY SCIENTIST WHO AGREED TO REMAIN WITH ME...

ALL THE OTHER SPECIALISTS OF THIS US ARMY SUPER-LABORATORY RAN LIKE RABBITS AS SOON AS THE CATACLYSM BEGAN. I ONLY MANAGED TO KEEP ONE, BUT I HAVE TO ADMIT HE'S REMARKABLE!

MR SCHROEDER...
MR SCHROEDER...

HE HATES BEING DISTURBED IN THE MIDDLE OF A DANGEROUS EXPERIMENT.

YES.. YES... WHAT NOW? I TOLD YOU BEFORE: JUST BECAUSE I'M YOUR PRISONER DOESN'T MEAN YOU SHOULD FEEL FREE TO PESTER ME EVERY FIVE MINUTES...

... I'M WILLING TO INVENT FOR YOU, BUT NOT CHITCHAT WITH YOU. UNDERSTOOD?... BESIDES, YOU HAVE NO CONVERSATIONAL SKILLS...

I SIMPLY WANTED TO INFORM YOU THAT THE DOCUMENTS FROM THE UNITED NATIONS HAD ARRIVED. AND... ER... MAY I ASK WHAT IMPORTANT EXPERIMENT YOU ARE CURRENTLY CONDUCTING?...

CAN'T YOU SEE? I'M MAKING SYNTHETIC WHISKY! WITH THE HORRIBLE SWILL YOUR ROBOTS COOK HERE...

... I NEED IT!

HA HA... OUR FRIEND SCHROEDER LOVES A GOOD JOKE!... BUT MAKE NO MISTAKE: HE'S UNDOUBTEDLY ONE OF THE MOST BRILLIANT SCIENTIFIC MINDS THAT EVER GRACED THE EARTH. AN ASSOCIATE WORTHY OF ME, IN TRUTH...

... AND YOU'VE ACTUALLY SEEN THE FIRST FRUITS OF OUR COLLABORATION: THESE ROBOTS THAT BROUGHT YOU HERE. STILL A BIT ROUGH, BUT ABSOLUTELY LOYAL. I SHOULD WARN YOU RIGHT AWAY THAT THEY ARE TUNED TO MY OWN BRAIN—AND OBEY ME ALONE...

ANYWAY, I DIDN'T BRING YOU HERE TO THREATEN YOU, SINCE YOU KNOW FULL WELL THAT YOU'RE TRAPPED. AS IT HAPPENS, I HAVE PLANS—AND I'M READY TO OFFER YOU A PART IN THEM. THE WORLD IS RIPE FOR ME TO GRAB AND SHAPE TO MY WILL. SCHROEDER IS PUTTING THE LAST TOUCHES TO SOME MILITARY EQUIPMENT WITH WHICH I INTEND TO IMPOSE MYSELF EASILY AS THE ONLY LEADER CAPABLE OF BRINGING THE EARTH OUT OF ANARCHY...

YOU, THE GANGSTER: I PROPOSE THAT YOU BECOME COMMANDER OF MY FUTURE TROOPS. AND YOU, VALERIAN, CAN BE MY RIGHT-HAND MAN FOR THIS COLOSSAL ENDEAVOUR. I'VE HAD THE OPPORTUNITY TO JUDGE YOUR SKILLS, BOTH OF YOU. WHAT DO YOU SAY?

HO HO... THIS SOUNDS INTERESTING...

YOU'VE GOT TO BE KIDDING!

YES, AMUSING... I'LL HAVE TO THINK ABOUT IT...

NO NEED! I HAD ANTICIPATED YOUR HESITATION, AND I THINK I HAVE A WAY TO HELP YOU THINK FAST. SO, PLEASE FOLLOW ME... WE'RE GOING TO CONDUCT A FUN, LITTLE APPLIED-PHYSICS EXPERIMENT ...

AT XOMBUL'S INVITATION, THE GROUP LEAVES THE LABORATORY AND HEADS DOWN INTO THE DEPTHS OF THE EARTH...

SUDDENLY, SCHROEDER PRETENDS TO TRIP...

YIKES! IT'S SLIPPERY HERE!!

... AND SLIPS A MYSTERIOUS OBJECT INTO VALERIAN'S HAND...

... TAKING ADVANTAGE OF THE CORRIDOR'S DARKNESS, HE WHISPERS HURRIEDLY...

THROW THIS DOWN WHEN I TELL YOU... WE MUST ESCAPE... I'M WITH YOU...

OH! SORRY...

... THEN, AS IF NOTHING HAD HAPPENED, THE TWO MEN WALK ON WITH THE OTHERS...

... AND COME TO A HUGE CAVE.

31

SEE THIS MACHINE HERE, VALERIAN?... THIS IS THE M.M.—THE FIRST MOLECULAR MINIATURISER!

SCHROEDER EVEN TESTED THE DEVICE BY SHRINKING A LIVE BUFFALO!!

LOOK AT IT. ISN'T IT CUTE? BUT THAT'S NOTHING! NEXT, I'M GOING TO TRY IT ON MAN—OR MORE ACCURATELY...

... WOMAN! YOUR FRIEND LAURELINE WILL BE MY FIRST TEST SUBJECT! YOU, TAKE HER TO THE PAD! SCHROEDER, TO YOUR CONSOLES.

DON'T WORRY, MISS! WE'RE JUST GOING TO MINIATURISE YOU NICELY. WE'LL HAVE TO DO IT IN SEVERAL STEPS; BUT ONCE YOU'RE THIS BIG AND I CAN KEEP YOU IN MY POCKET AT ALL TIMES, YOUR FRIEND VALERIAN WILL BE VERY COOPERATIVE! HA! HA!

IF I TRY TO DO SOMETHING NOW, I'LL BE FRIED BEFORE I CAN EVEN BLINK.

IN A STRANGELY MURKY LIGHT...

... LAURELINE BEGINS...

... TO SHRINK...

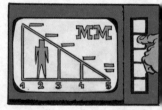

... STAGE BY STAGE...

32

... SUDDENLY, SCHROEDER CRIES OUT...

NOW, VALERIAN!

CLING

STRUCK BY THE DEAFENING SOUND WAVES THAT FLOOD THE CABIN, XOMBUL AND THE ROBOTS BEGIN THRASHING ABOUT WILDLY.

AND AMIDST THE GENERAL CONFUSION, AFTER HAVING SHUT OFF THE M.M...

MM
STOP
1 2 3 4 5

... VALERIAN RUSHES TO LAURELINE'S AID.

LAURELINE!

MEANWHILE, INSIDE THE CABIN, THE INFERNAL DIN IS STILL RINGING.

THAT'S ENOUGH, NOW! BRING THAT THING DOWN BEFORE WE GO DEAF!

LAURELINE!!!

HOW ARE YOU FEELING, LAURELINE?... TALK TO ME; SAY SOMETHING.

8A

BUT I AM TALKING TO YOU, YOU IDIOT! I CAN'T SHOUT ANY LOUDER!!! DO SOMETHING! HELP ME! I'VE HAD ENOUGH... THIS KIND OF THINGS ALWAYS HAPPENS TO THE GIRLS!

MEANWHILE...

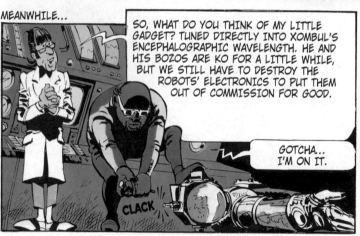

SO, WHAT DO YOU THINK OF MY LITTLE GADGET? TUNED DIRECTLY INTO XOMBUL'S ENCEPHALOGRAPHIC WAVELENGTH. HE AND HIS BOZOS ARE KO FOR A LITTLE WHILE, BUT WE STILL HAVE TO DESTROY THE ROBOTS' ELECTRONICS TO PUT THEM OUT OF COMMISSION FOR GOOD.

GOTCHA... I'M ON IT.

CLACK

FINALLY...

THERE, IT'S DONE. THEY'RE ALL BRAIN DEAD NOW!

WHAT ABOUT ME? WHAT BECOMES OF ME NOW, HUH?!

HMM... IT'S AN ANNOYANCE, OF COURSE. THE M.M. ONLY WORKS ONE WAY...

... BUT SINCE THE PROCEDURE WASN'T COMPLETED, YOU WILL GROW BACK TO YOUR NORMAL SIZE LITTLE BY LITTLE. IT SHOULD ACTUALLY BE QUICK...

YOU SEE, EVERYTHING WILL BE FINE!

ANYWAY, WE HAVE TO GET OUT OF HERE. LET'S GET BACK TO THE HELICOPTER; THAT'S THE EASIEST WAY! SUN RAE, YOU GRAB XOMBUL—WE'RE LEAVING...

WHOA! YOU'RE HAPPY BECAUSE YOU CAUGHT YOUR PREY—BUT ME, I'M STAYING HERE...

8B

OK, YOU STAY. I HAVEN'T FORGOTTEN OUR AGREEMENT: YOU KEEP THE GADGETS AND I HAVE XOMBUL!

SEE YOU, AND GOOD LUCK!

ER... I'M COMING WITH Y...

NO YOU'RE NOT! YOU'RE STAYING HERE WITH ME. I NEED SOME TUTORING IN PHYSICS AND CHEMISTRY...

A BIT LATER...

I DON'T LIKE LEAVING SCHROEDER. BUT WE MUST GET TO BRASILIA! I DON'T KNOW WHAT THE RANGE OF THAT CHOPPER IS, BUT WE'RE BOUND TO FIND A WAY TO KEEP GOING...

SURE...

... AND THEN, MAYBE ONCE WE'RE BACK IN GALAXITY, YOU COULD FIND A FEW MINUTES IN YOUR BUSY SCHEDULE TO TRY AND GIVE ME BACK MY NORMAL SIZE, RIGHT?

BUT... IT'S NOT MY FAULT IF... HEY, WHAT'S THAT NOISE BEHIND US?

YOU COULD HAVE WAITED FOR ME! IT'S A GOOD THING I MANAGED TO LOSE YOUR FRIEND INSIDE THE MAINFRAME...

THEN LET'S KEEP GOING. I CAN FEEL XOMBUL STARTING TO MOVE...

BUT, AT THE EXIT...

CURSES! THEY WERE TOO FAR; MY INVENTION DIDN'T HAVE ANY EFFECT ON THEM THROUGH THAT MUCH ROCK...

BY VENUS! I'D FORGOTTEN ABOUT THESE GUYS!

LET ME GO, YOU BRUTISH OAF!

STOP SQUIRMING LIKE THAT DOWN THERE; I'M GOING TO LOSE MY GRIP! VALERIAN, MAKE HIM STOP!

OH, ENOUGH, YOU TWO! IF YOU THINK IT'S EASY TO CARRY YOU AROUND!

35

WE CAN GET TO THE MESA THIS WAY...

XOMBUL, STAY PUT OR I'LL KNOCK YOU OUT!

STOP BOM

THERE, HE'S QUIET NOW! HANG ON, LAURELINE, WE'RE RUNNING!

VALERIAN!!!

VALERIAN! YOU'VE BEEN HIT!

IT'S NOTHING, A SURFACE BURN! TOO BAD ABOUT XOMBUL! WE HAVE TO ESCAPE QUICKLY! THEY WANT US DEAD, NOW!

WHAT ARE YOU WAITING FOR?! GO AFTER THEM!

AND ATOP THE BARREN MESA, A LONG RACE BEGINS...

36

NOW, WHAT ON EARTH IS THIS CONTRAPTION?

A SMALL ANTI-GRAVITY VEHICLE. FORTUNATELY FOR US, I HAVEN'T FINISHED WORKING ON IT. IT MOVES AT A SNAIL'S PACE...

THE FLIGHT CONTINUES. STUMBLING AT EVERY STEP, VALERIAN HEADS DOWN INTO A MAZE OF CANYONS...

WE CAN'T GO ON LIKE THIS; IT'D BE MADNESS! THESE MACHINES ARE TIRELESS, WHEREAS WE...

LET'S HIDE OVER THERE...

SOON...

WE HAVE A CHANCE. THEIR RADAR IS AN OLD ONE I SCROUNGED UP, AND IT ISN'T MUCH GOOD... LET'S HOPE THEY'LL GO ON INTO THE MAIN CANYON...

SHHH... WHAT'S WITH YOU? MUST YOU MOVE AROUND LIKE THAT?

NUTS! I'M NOT MOVING— I'M GROWING !!!

AFTER A FEW ANXIOUS MINUTES...

THAT'S IT... THEY'RE GONE!

I LOOK LIKE A SCARECROW NOW!

STRANGE!... YOUR CLOTHES MUST HAVE GROWN SLOWER THAN YOUR BODY. COME ON; WE'LL TAKE THE OTHER CANYON...

THE GROUP RESUMES ITS TREK...

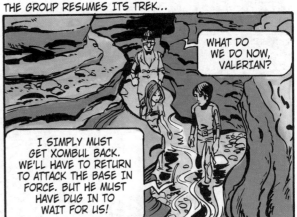

WHAT DO WE DO NOW, VALERIAN?

I SIMPLY MUST GET XOMBUL BACK. WE'LL HAVE TO RETURN TO ATTACK THE BASE IN FORCE. BUT HE MUST HAVE DUG IN TO WAIT FOR US!

ALL NIGHT LONG, IN UNNATURAL HEAT, THEY WALK ON...

HOW DO YOU FEEL, LAURELINE?

WELL, I'M BEAT...

OH, I'M A BIG GIRL NOW... YOU'RE THE ONE WHO NEEDS ATTENTION, WITH YOUR WOUND...

FINALLY, AT DAWN; BEFORE A LANDSCAPE SCARRED BY DEEP CREVICES, LEFT BY THE EARTHQUAKES THAT HAVE DEVASTATED THE REGION...

DOWN THERE! A MILITARY BASE! IT LOOKS ABANDONED...

A FEW HOURS LATER, AT THE EDGE OF YELLOWSTONE. IN A PROVIDENTIAL JEEP, SALVAGED AND LOADED TO OVERFLOWING WITH VARIOUS WEAPONS AND AMMO...

WE'RE GETTING NEAR... I WONDER IF THERE'S AN ALARM SYSTEM MONITORING THE PARK'S BORDERS.

THERE WAS ONE WHEN THE BASE WAS ACTIVE. XOMBUL MUST STILL BE USING IT.

ENJOY A VISIT TO BEAUTIFUL YELLOWSTONE National Park 10 miles

GOOD! LET'S TAKE ADVANTAGE OF THE DECREASE IN TREMORS TO PROVOKE HIM... I DON'T THINK THE ROBOTS WILL SURVIVE A BAZOOKA.

IT'S RISKY, BUT I DON'T SEE WHAT ELSE TO DO. ANYWAY, WE MUST ACT QUICKLY. THIS PATCH OF SEISMIC CALM IS NOT A GOOD SIGN. SOME DISASTER WORSE THAN ALL THE PREVIOUS ONES IS IN THE MAKING...

THAT'S IT; WE'VE CROSSED INTO THE PARK...

LET'S KEEP OUR EYES PEELED. IF THE ALARM SYSTEM IS STILL WORKING, XOMBUL SHOULDN'T TAKE LONG TO SHOW HIS HAND. IT'S A PITY WE DON'T KNOW WHERE THE DANGER WILL COME FROM...

NOW ENTERING YELLO National

IN THE OPPRESSIVE ATMOSPHERE, THE CAR FORGES ON CAREFULLY, EVERYONE INSIDE ON HIGH ALERT. SUDDENLY...

XOMBUL!!

WELL, WE ASKED FOR IT! LET'S FIND SOME COVER!!!

HURRY!

AND WHILE LAURELINE BEGINS TO FIRE IN BURSTS...

... AS LAURELINE, HER AIM OBSTRUCTED BY THE ROCK OVERHANG, CEASES FIRE FOR A MOMENT, A HEAVY, FOREBODING SILENCE DESCENDS...

... MEANWHILE, UNDER THE STILL-CIRCLING AIRCRAFT...

WHAT THE DEVIL IS THIS?

THE BUBBLES!!! THE VILLAIN— HE REMEMBERED! LAURELINE, SHOOT!!!

LAURELINE SCORES SEVERAL HITS, BUT THE DROP CONTINUES STEADILY...

THE BUBBLES?

ANOTHER ONE OF MY INVENTIONS: PRISON-BUBBLES! SHOOT THEM BEFORE THEY FORM; OTHERWISE...

OTHERWISE WHAT?

TAKATAKATA

TOO LATE!

... SLOWLY, THE BUBBLES SWALLOW THEIR VICTIMS...

BY SPACE! WE'RE TRAPPED!!!

SAVE YOUR EFFORTS, VALERIAN...

... I MUST SAY, THE PRISON-BUBBLE IS ONE OF MY MOST EXCELLENT IDEAS. A PACIFIC WEAPON, REALLY... AND IMPOSSIBLE TO DEFEAT. A SMALL, SHAPED FORCE FIELD. ALL XOMBUL HAS TO DO NOW IS BRING US BACK REMOTELY TO THE BASE.

WELL... CONGRATULATIONS, SCHROEDER... YOU COULD HAVE TOLD US ABOUT THESE!

YES, WE'RE DONE FOR!

XOMBUL MUST HAVE GOTTEN BACK TO THE LAB. HIS AIRCRAFT WASN'T TOO SERIOUSLY DAMAGED...

GENTLY, THE BUBBLES FLOAT TOWARDS THE BASE...

BUT SUDDENLY, ACROSS A CONVULSING LANDSCAPE, THE VERY EARTH SEEMS TO CATCH ON FIRE...

LOOK! THE ERUPTIONS ARE BEGINNING!

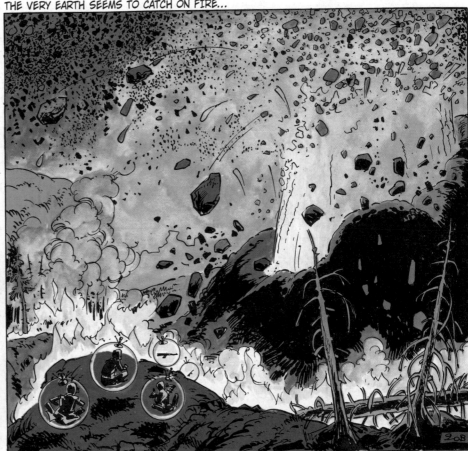

THE PRISON-BUBBLES, OUT OF CONTROL, GO OFF THEIR STRAIGHT LINE ITINERARY AND ARE SOON DRIFTING ALONG A RIVER OF LAVA...

HALF-CONSCIOUS, THE PRISONERS ARE TOSSED AROUND BY THE CATACLYSMIC BREATH THAT SWEEPS THE GROUND WITH VOLCANIC ASH...

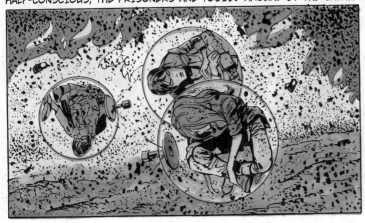

MUCH LATER, AFTER THE ERUPTIONS HAVE DECREASED IN INTENSITY, THE THREE BUBBLES COME TO A GENTLE REST ON A CARPET OF HOT ASH. THEN THEY OPEN, AND...

WHAT HAPPENED?

SOMEONE—OR SOMETHING—SHUT OFF THE FORCE FIELD. WE WERE LUCKY IT DIDN'T HAPPEN ABOVE THE LAVA!

HMM! YOUR BUBBLES ACTUALLY SAVED US FROM DISASTER!

WE HAVE TO GET BACK TO THE BASE... IF IT'S STILL THERE. ANYTHING RATHER THAN STAY OUT IN THIS HELL!

AS IT HAPPENS, WE WENT AROUND IN CIRCLES. THE ENTRANCE TO THE TUNNEL IS UP THERE... A SHORT HALF-HOUR WALK...

SOON...

A LITTLE LATER...

AND MANY HALF-HOURS LATER!!!

MY LAB!!

SUN RAE!

THAT'S RIGHT! IT WAS I WHO FREED YOU AFTER I SAW ON THE SCREEN THAT YOU WERE IN LESS DANGER. IT TOOK ME SOME TIME TO FIGURE OUT HOW THE MACHINE WORKED!.. BUT, HERE YOU ARE AT LAST!

MY LAB! COMPLETELY WRECKED! OH, THE HUMANITY...

ERM... OUR RELATIONS ENDED UP BEING VERY DISAPPOINTING, YOU KNOW. IN ANY CASE, HE BOLTED!

WHAT ABOUT XOMBUL?

WHAT?!

HOURS AGO. I WAS HIDING NEAR THE ROCKET, BECAUSE OF THOSE DAMNED ROBOTS. I SAW XOMBUL RUSH TO IT AT THE FIRST TREMOR, IGNITE THE ENGINE AND.... GOODBYE!

THE ROCKET! WHAT ROCKET??

THAT ROCKET THERE!

... THE PERSONAL ROCKET OF THE PRESIDENT OF THE UNITED STATES! HE WAS SUPPOSED TO RETREAT HERE IN CASE OF A NUCLEAR ATTACK, AND THEN LEAVE THE EARTH FOR AN ORBITAL STATION IF ALL WAS LOST.

AND XOMBUL ENDED UP USING IT!

AND WHERE IS THAT ROCKET NOW?

IT WAS ON AUTOPILOT. WHAT YOU'RE SEEING HERE IS A LIVE FEED FROM THE AUTOMATIC CAMERAS ONBOARD THE ORBITAL REFUGE...

YEAH, XOMBUL'S BEEN BUZZING AROUND UP THERE FOR A WHILE!

LOOK! HE TOOK THE DOCUMENTS LOOTED FROM NEW YORK WITH HIM!!

WHAT IS HE WORKING ON?!

THAT I'D LIKE TO KNOW! I WAS AWARE THAT THERE WAS SOME SCIENTIFIC EQUIPMENT UP THERE. BUT IT WAS ALL "TOP SECRET"! EVEN I DIDN'T KNOW WHAT IT WAS ALL ABOUT!

BUT WHAT CAN WE DO?! WE HAVE TO GO GET HIM!!

... OH, YEAH? AND HOW?... HANGING FROM A KITE?...

PFF... GIVE ME A SHOUT WHEN YOU FIGURE OUT SOMETHING...

EVERYONE IS LOST IN DARK THOUGHTS. ON THE SCREENS, OCCASIONALLY BLURRED BY THE TREMORS OF THE EARTH'S CRUST, XOMBUL—THOUSANDS OF MILES AWAY AND UNAWARE THAT HE'S BEING OBSERVED—IS HARD AT WORK.

YOU DON'T LET THINGS GET TO YOU, DO YOU?

BAH! WE'RE STILL BETTER OFF IN HERE THAN OUTSIDE—CAN YOU HEAR ALL THE ERUPTIONS?

SUDDENLY...

WHAT'S THIS THING HERE?!

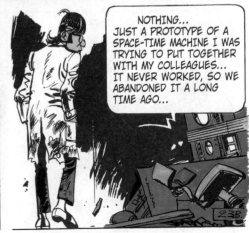

NOTHING... JUST A PROTOTYPE OF A SPACE-TIME MACHINE I WAS TRYING TO PUT TOGETHER WITH MY COLLEAGUES... IT NEVER WORKED, SO WE ABANDONED IT A LONG TIME AGO...

 **ARE YOU THINKING WHAT I'M THINKING, THEN?**

YES! BUT IT'S IMPOSSIBLE! THE FIRST MACHINE WAS INVENTED IN 2314, AND WE'RE IN 1986! SCHROEDER MIGHT BE A GENIUS, BUT STILL...

 **THIS THING ISN'T THAT GREAT!... THE ENGINEERING WILL NEED A LOT OF HELP.**

IT'S WORTH A TRY—IF WE MODIFY ALL THE CIRCUITRY!

HUH, WHAT...?

 **WHAT ARE YOU TRYING TO DO?? YOU DON'T KNOW THE FIRST THING ABOUT THE MECHANICS OF SPACE-TIME...**

MAYBE TWO OR THREE SCIENTISTS IN THE WORLD COULD...

AS IT HAPPENS, I DABBLE A BIT!... AND I LOVE TO TINKER... LEAVE US TO IT, NOW. YOU HEAD DOWN TOO, SUN RAE!

OK, OK...

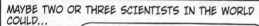

AND SHORTLY AFTERWARDS...

... A STRANGE PARALLEL RACE BEGINS...

HOW'S XOMBUL DOING?

IT LOOKS LIKE HE'S USING THE DOCUMENTS TO DO SOME FINE-TUNING!

OK, I SEE WHAT'S WRONG. IT WAS ACTUALLY THE SUBJECT OF MY ENTRANCE EXAM TO THE SPATIO-TEMPORAL SERVICE... EASY FOR US, BUT IMPOSSIBLE FOR PEOPLE OF THE 20TH CENTURY TO SOLVE! LET'S GET TO IT—WRITE DOWN: ...

GO AHEAD!

244

I'LL CHECK THE STATION'S COORDINATES. IN THE MEANTIME, FIND US SOME SPACESUITS AND BRING THE OTHERS...

OK! THERE'S BOUND TO BE SOMETHING LIKE THAT IN A BASE LIKE THIS!

SOON...

I'VE GOT EVERYTHING... YOU?

ALL DONE! IT'S UP TO YOU NOW, LAURELINE!

YOU'RE MAD! IT CAN'T WORK, IT'S A MATHEMATICAL IMPOSSIBILITY!

BAH! IF WE STAY HERE, WE'RE DONE FOR ANYWAY!

WE RISK INSTANT DISINTEGRATION! I'M WARNING Y...OUCH!

 POK POK

FINALLY, AFTER SOME HASTY LAST-MINUTE PREPARATIONS...

POOR SCHROEDER, POOR SUN RAE... UNPLEASANT METHODS, BUT WE COULDN'T SIMPLY LEAVE THEM HERE...

... NO MORE THAN WE COULD LET THEM SEE WHERE WE'RE GOING! COME ON, HURRY! TIME TO GO—EVERYTHING IS COLLAPSING HERE...

OK! EVERYTHING'S SET. IGNITION!

24B

FOR THE FIRST TIME IN EARTH'S HISTORY, HUMAN BEINGS DIVE INTO THE VORTEX OF SPACE-TIME...

... INSTANTANEOUSLY, VALERIAN AND LAURELINE FIND THEMSELVES FLOATING IN SPACE, NEAR THE SECRET STATION WHERE XOMBUL HAS TAKEN REFUGE, THOUSANDS OF MILES FROM EARTH...

IT WORKED!!! I CAN TELL YOU NOW: I DIDN'T REALLY TRUST THIS JURY-RIGGED THING OF YOURS...

ME, NEITHER— BUT WE'RE NOT DONE YET! LOOK AFTER OUR FRIENDS; I'M GOING AFTER XOMBUL.

I'VE BEEN AFTER HIM FOR SO LONG...

OPTING FOR THE DIRECT APPROACH, VALERIAN ENTERS THE STATION THROUGH THE HATCH...

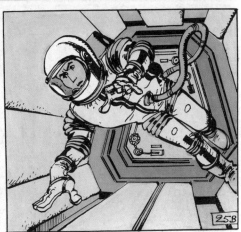

AND...

IT'S OVER, XOMBUL!!! I'M TAKING YOU BACK TO GALAXITY!

VALERIAN!!!

I HAD A HUNCH ABOUT WHAT YOU'D COME TO THE 20TH CENTURY TO FIND: THE FIRST TIME MACHINE. TOUGH LUCK: I'M THE ONE WHO FOUND IT! JUST LOOK AT HOW I GOT HERE... YOU SHOULD HAVE PAID MORE ATTENTION TO SCHROEDER'S DISCARD PILE... EVEN HIS FAILURES ARE IMPRESSIVE!

THAT'S TRUE... BUT HERE, I HAD EVERYTHING AT HAND: THE PLANS RECOVERED FROM THE UN WERE THOSE OF A SPACE-TIME MACHINE THAT THE GREATEST SCIENTISTS HAD WORKED ON. I JUST FINISHED BUILDING IT...

... AND I WAS ABOUT TO RETURN TO EARTH. WITH MY MACHINE AND MY WEAPONS, I COULD HAVE SAVED HUMANITY... TRAVELLED THROUGH HISTORY AT WILL... CHANGED WHAT I DEEMED BAD... BROUGHT ORDER! I, ALONE, COULD HAVE GUIDED THIS INSANE WORLD TOWARDS A GLORIOUS FUTURE! AND TO THINK MY MACHINE WILL NEVER BE USED...

26

SUDDENLY...

HA! HA!... YOU HAVEN'T HEARD THE LAST FROM ME!

DON'T DO THIS—ARE YOU CRAZY?!!
A MACHINE FROM THE 20TH CENTURY **CANNOT** WORK!...

... DISREGARDING VALERIAN'S WARNING, XOMBUL ATTEMPTS TO LAUNCH HIMSELF THROUGH SPACE-TIME...

THE FOOL!!!

... FOR A SPLIT SECOND, HIS MACHINE—UNABLE TO MAKE THE JUMP—MATERIALISES OVER THE STATION'S RING.

BUT...

26

IN THE ETERNAL SILENCE OF SPACE, BEFORE VALERIAN'S HORRIFIED EYES, VEHICLE AND PASSENGER ARE MERCILESSLY DESTROYED BEFORE LIFTING AWAY AS SCATTERED DEBRIS...

OU LOST, XOMBUL! AND IT WAS YOUR OWN FAULT: YOU DIDN'T KNOW ANYTHING ABOUT SPACE-TIME MACHINES!!! ALL RIGHT, NOW'S OT THE TIME TO GET EMOTIONAL. MISSION ACCOMPLISHED. WE SHOULD GET BACK TO EARTH...

STILL... A QUICK LOOK AT ALL THIS!

AFTER A QUICK INSPECTION...

THESE IMAGES! THESE ARE THE DOCUMENTS I WAS SHOWN IN GALAXITY BEFORE I LEFT... NOW I UNDERSTAND!

IN SEVERAL CENTURIES, WHAT STARTED ME ON THIS MISSION WILL BE DISCOVERED HERE. THEN EVERYTHING IS SORTED. THE CIRCLE IS COMPLETE...

A LITTLE LATER...

DID YOU SEE WHAT HAPPENED TO XOMBUL?

YES... IT WASN'T YOUR FAULT. COME ON—THE MACHINE IS READY TO REMATERIALISE IN BRASILIA...

LET'S TRUST THIS BUCKET OF BOLTS ONE MORE TIME, THEN... BEFORE OUR PASSENGERS WAKE UP.

IF IT FAILS, THE POOR DEVILS WILL NEVER EVEN KNOW...

SOON AFTER, NEAR BRASILIA...

OW! MY HEAD... WHERE ARE WE?

WHAT HAPPENED? WHERE' XOMBUL...?

IT'S ALL OVER! COME THIS V I'LL EXPLAIN... LAURELINE, Y KNOW WHAT TO DO...

LISTEN, SCHROEDER, YOU'RE PROBABLY ONE OF THE FEW MINDS IN THE 20TH CENTURY ABLE TO ACCEPT WHAT I'M ABOUT TO SAY... AND TO KEEP IT TO YOURSELF. THIS MACHINE YOU JUST CLIMBED OUT OF? IT JUST MADE A JUMP THROUGH SPACE-TIME—AND I MYSELF AM A TRAVELLER FROM THE FUTURE...

COME ON! THAT'S IMPOSSIBLE! ALL THE CALCULATIONS SHOW THAT...

YES... EXCEPT THAT THE CALCULATIONS ARE WRONG... I CAN'T TELL YOU MORE THAN THAT—IT'S UP TO THE PEOPLE OF TODAY'S EARTH TO SOLVE THE PROBLEM. GO TO BRASILIA, SCHROEDER... THERE, YOU WILL JOIN THE GREATEST SCIENTISTS OF THIS TIME... AND YOU HAVE YOUR WORK CUT OUT FOR YOU!

AT LEAST LET ME HAVE A LOOK AT THE MACHINE!

LOOK AT THE MACHINE? GO AHEAD. UNFORTUNATELY, I PUT IT BACK THE WAY YOU'D LEFT IT...

YOU VANDALS! YOU RETROGRADES!!! IT MIGHT TAKE HUNDREDS OF YEARS TO FIND...

MAYBE!... BUT, BEING FROM THE FUTURE DOESN'T GI US THE RIGHT TO CHANGE THE PAST.

AT LAST...

THEY'RE OFF TO BRASILIA... I WONDER WHAT THEY'LL FIND THERE...

OH, WE CAN TRUST THEM! THEY'RE BOTH THE RESOURCEFUL TYPE—AND EARTH NEEDS PEOPLE LIKE THAT!

LATER, AT THE UNIVERSITY OF BRASILIA...

... THANK YOU FOR YOUR WELCOME, GENTLEMEN! I DO BELIEVE I HAVE A FEW RESEARCH PROJECTS TO PROPOSE... LET'S GET TO WORK!

... IN THE CITY'S UNDERGROUND...

UNDERSTOOD, BOYS? WE CAN TAKE CONTRO OF THE CITY IN TWO DAYS. HERE'S MY PLA LET'S GET TO WORK!

... AND NEARBY:

THERE'S THE ENTRANCE TO THE RELAY... LET'S HEAD BACK TO GALAXITY!

HMM... MAYBE WE COULD MAKE A LITTLE TEMPORAL SIDE TRIP BEFORE RETURNING TO THE 28TH CENTURY... I KNOW THEM. WE WON'T HAVE BEEN BACK FOR AN HOUR BEFORE THEY'LL SEND US BACK TO WORK...

SCRIPT: P. CHRISTI DRAWING: J.C. MEZIER

THE END

69